BOA
EDITIONS LTD

Flare, Corona

Flare, Corona

Jeannine Hall Gailey

AMERICAN POETS CONTINUUM SERIES, NO. 201

BOA EDITIONS, LTD. ☼ ROCHESTER, NY ☼ 2023

First Edition
23 24 25 26 7 6 5 4 3 2 1

For information about permission to reuse any material from this book, please contact The Permissions Company at www.permissionscompany.com or e-mail permdude@gmail.com.

Publications by BOA Editions, Ltd.—a not-for-profit corporation under section 501 (c) (3) of the United States Internal Revenue Code—are made possible with funds from a variety of sources, including public funds from the Literature Program of the National Endowment for the Arts; the New York State Council on the Arts, a state agency; and the County of Monroe, NY. Private funding sources include the Max and Marian Farash Charitable Foundation; the Mary S. Mulligan Charitable Trust; the Rochester Area Community Foundation; the Ames-Amzalak Memorial Trust in memory of Henry Ames, Semon Amzalak, and Dan Amzalak; the LGBT Fund of Greater Rochester; and contributions from many individuals nationwide. See Colophon on page 112 for special individual acknowledgments.

Cover Art and Design: Sandy Knight
Interior Design and Composition: Isabella Madeira
BOA Logo: Mirko

BOA Editions books are available electronically through BookShare, an online distributor offering Large-Print, Braille, Multimedia Audio Book, and Dyslexic formats, as well as through e-readers that feature text to speech capabilities.

Cataloging-in-Publication Data is available from the Library of Congress.

NYSCA

BOA Editions, Ltd.
250 North Goodman Street, Suite 306
Rochester, NY 14607
www.boaeditions.org
A. Poulin, Jr., Founder (1938-1996)

NATIONAL
ENDOWMENT
for the ARTS
arts.gov

Contents

Post-Life

Harbingers

Blood Moon

Corona

Post-Life

Irradiate

As a child I was radiant.
The land grew irradiated corn and roses,
tomatoes large and abundant. Swallows and catfish
carrying the isotopes into the water and woods.
The sun rose each day, while the shadows
of trees concealed government laboratories
where my father worked.
I grew up listening to the tap click
of the Geiger counter. I grew up listening
to clicks on the phone line.
I was still innocent. Irradiated.
To blast with radiation—to sterilize
food, medical equipment, a person.
I was waiting for a message from the sky.

I knew what it meant to illuminate—
the fall of light in a painting, or through an old window
that irradiated a field of flowers, of the face of someone
you loved—to bring the full beauty of something to the surface.
I was irradiated by the gentle glow
of the computer screen, by the microwave,
by the sun growing brighter each spring,
dimmer each fall. I meant I was full of
radiation. I meant I was full of light.
I meant I could give birth to nothing
but light.

Calamity

Your family is coming over for Thanksgiving.
Even worse, it's snowing.

Headless robots are playing soccer with your soul.
UFOs have been sighted overhead.

A meteor is definitely heading straight for you.
It might miss, but then again.

Tonight a city is being decimated by Godzilla,
or was it a bunch of genetically-engineered dinosaurs?

Either way, I hope you're lizard-friendly.
Tonight you have to give a speech

and that girl who hated you in third grade
will be in the audience. What have I ever done

to deserve this? the prophet asks, tearing his robes
in the desert. God responds: how long you got?

A plague of egrets, of eaglets, of egress.
A black hole has just opened up and it is

already swallowing someone else's sun.
Did you see the team play last night? A travesty.

Someone is always preaching about doomsday.
Who are you wearing? Because tonight

your life will be required of you. Grab a bag,
a sword, a water bottle. Go out swinging.

On Being Told You're Dying, but Not Quite Believing It

Because around you, the mortal world is always dying,
that banana you left behind at breakfast and that calf

you just saw mooing for its mother in the pasture.
Oh, vaccines and antibiotics and moisturizers can only hold

death at bay for so long, its breath on us a push towards the door.
Grab your coat, death says, get ready for adventure!

Let's play a game in which no one ever dies,
all serene and ageless—a universe of unicorns, dynamic as glass,

impossible to impassion. After all, angels have no investment
in the living, in the dirty nature of breeding and birth,

in our grubby hands clutching at the soil from beginning to end,
as if to stay a little longer. You remember volunteering

in the Children's Hospital ward, little faces as sunny and smiling
towards death as they were towards popsicles, or a new set of crayons,

while their parents looked on, afraid and weepy.
And anyway, is there any way really to prepare for that goodbye,

to send your body…elsewhere, to break down quietly? We can choose
to time our sorrow. I believe in today, this apple that isn't quite ripe yet,

this poem that isn't finished, a bed rumpled with my husband's still
sleeping form, my lungs still breathing, my fingers still on this page.

Not Dead but Post-Life

Like a post-doc post-graduate student,
I'm looking forward to being—not dead—
but post-life. Post-life, with post-it notes
to remind people *Look, I was here.*
Post-life, I'll be lighter and all my vanities
and anxieties extinguished. Post-life, my romantic life
will resolve into fond memory, blurry videos
where the real me used to be, fuzzy enough
to distort wrinkles or asymmetries into oblivion.
My internet profile will live on without me,
probably more popular than before. Post-life
my books will become better sellers, my professional
self easier to swallow, harder to critique.
Not dead but post-life, I will leave this weak and fragile
body behind, become a beam of light
in a field of daffodils, float, a paper lantern, into the sky,
free of tethers, tassels, telephones, trappings of the old me
falling away, a road-trip of destiny. Drop me a note,
will you? Drop in! Post-life will be nothing
but firefly freedom, a freefall into formlessness, finally.

Have I Mentioned Lately

that every story I tell is an apocalypse story?
That every time I turn on the news

or look out the window, something else is on fire.
I've stockpiled water. I know all the exits.

I've already said my farewells. But I'm not ready.
I haven't yet established my own city of lights.

I haven't even built a city of roses. It's just me,
here, surrounded by my books, quiet. Yesterday

a meteor streaked by my house. The sonic boom
shook the earth. I saw the tail of flame

and thought, there goes the neighborhood.
I read that the ice is melting, seas rising, solar

flares reaching for us. Still we keep flying higher.
We keep crafting escapades. In the face of calamity,

we keep cupcakes. In the blackout, a beacon of light:
that candle you lit in the window. Saying goodbye

is harder than you think. You look behind you,
just a second, before the flash, before the pillar of salt.

Failure, 2016

I failed to die (as they said I might) this year.
I watched the icons of my teen years drop one by one though,
magical in their makeup and costumes, Bowie and Prince

and Princess Leia, all glitter and smartass. I watched the election
with tears in my eyes while others cheered.
I spent a lot of time in hospitals, not writing, waiting

for the other shoe to drop. I spent too much time handwringing.
I spent time planting lavender that I wasn't sure
I would live to see bloom. I bought a blue-eyed kitten.

I took pictures of trees in the wind.
Failures were many—lost voices, lost crowds, wandering
in the wrong directions. We've lost our sense of smell.

All the signs are there. We've barely touched our eggs.
Our memories aren't what they used to be. Our hair
not as bright. Our hands shake when they should be steady.

America lost a bit of its shine. Britons yelled at us
in the street to *go back home*. But where did we
come from? Wasn't it on your boats?

I've forgotten now, English, Gaelic, African, French,
Creole, Spanish, Italian, Latin, ancient Greek: so many languages
scratched into the dust, into rusty iron pages.

They're breaking down. Soon we will all speak emoji,
happy or sad faces, angry tongues or devil horns.
We failed to launch as a nation. I failed to organize

my closet, my office is a mess of papers I can't leave
to anyone. A painting on my wall of a fox, its eyes glowing,
fixed on the grey horizon. It haunts me, with its wall of poppies.

Where did my nerve break down? What particular cell betrayed me?
Are your families fracturing, your synapses leaking?
Look to the future—perhaps that glow you see isn't fire, but sunrise.

Self-Portrait as Murder Mystery

A luxury liner on the high seas loses contact
during a storm; a train is trapped in perilous
mountains by an avalanche of snow.
A cabin on an island when the power goes out.
The passengers are suddenly isolated
and everyone is a suspect; the kindly nanny
may be an American spy, the priest
who is certainly an assassin,
everyone else is a magician or a Nazi scientist.
Every detail oozes with malice;
a waiter who pours the suspect tea
into a cup with studied grace,
a newspaper headline that announces bombings
in an obscure European town.
The anarchist dragged out to be shot
by the ever-present police. There are
so many coincidences and red herrings
that every missing ring, every lost suitcase,
inherits charged importance.
What you love about these stories
is the shoestring lace that ties everything
together. The trail of clues, like pebbles
you could follow home, to make order out of chaos.
How we long for our lives to be as easily solved.
What a surprise for the reader when the murderer
turns out to be the narrator herself, the way
she slipped out of the room at the right time
with the gun, the way she misled everyone
with her kind smile and rhinestone cane.

The Summer of Bombs

It was a summer of hydrogen bombs,
eclipses, earthquakes, hurricanes, wild fires.
We were not exaggerating. The world
was covered in smoke. Remember the shooter
on that boat on the island? It was the summer
everything blew up. Including us.
The embers of my neurology fell into place
like video game aliens about to explode.
You couldn't understand, you couldn't see.
I could do so much less. The wind smelled
like bullets all the time. I couldn't keep down fluids.
You couldn't keep down your voice.
I needed help. You wanted out.
It seemed to me that every man was trying
to shake the earth to loosen our grip on things
or maybe that was Mother Nature trying to shake us off.
I certainly couldn't hold on when the storm came.
It was lights out for me. The bombs in the air
had already taken hold in my mind.
They had already landed in me, exploded,
leaving wreckage. There was no recovery,
no map to the future. The sun angry, the sea intolerant.
The atoms had shifted, irreparable.

Self-Portrait as Radioactive Girl

I've been eating poisoned apples
unknowingly my whole life.

In my portrait, my hair glows green
along with my skin-tight catsuit,

a mask over eyes that may or may not
emit an otherworldly blue glow.

In my bones, organs, skin, I've been storing
all of America's dark secrets

from exposure—Cesium 137, Iodine 131.
Man-made isotopes, created for one purpose—death.

My medical history is pure science fiction,
nuclear accidents and robot parts.

Nuclear energy is clean and safe, the men in dark suits
will tell you, the same men who tapped our phones

and lurked in corners around Oak Ridge, always on the alert
for spies. They know exactly what happens

to the children of these workers, eating the produce
and milk grown from earth sown with nuclear waste,

contaminated groundwater, radioactive dust.
Lung and liver and brain bloom with lesions,

mysterious in origin, and doctors have told me
I am like the X-Men, a mutant of incredible origin

with no statistics to match my patterns.
At the end, I explode a pure blue flame,

my radioactive atoms returning to the earth and sky.

They Are Waiting

For blood work. For a sign.
For fancy X-rays that will map out
which parts of me went wrong, and where.
You can't travel to me.

They are waiting for me to straighten up, fly right
into the waiting V in a sky of snow geese.
They are waiting for me to get better. Me too.
While we wait, the pink tulips begin drooping,

the weight of their petals shedding in the dark.
Me too. They are waiting, but I can't tell them
what they want to hear. They can't hear me
when my body sings, vibrates a melody

tense and uneven. What was it you said to me once?
They don't have statistics for people like me?
No map. No statistics. No hard facts.
So don't count on me to give you the exposé,

the real story. Inside my mouth I keep the whispers
of ghosts. White feathers begin to fall, heavy, like the tulips.
If you wait long enough, maybe I'll reveal the trick to survival
in a body humming with death. I'm waiting too.

Self-Portrait as Weather Report

After that high-pressure system swept through,
you gave way to flooding and severe storms.
You couldn't push all the way to the East Coast,
so you remained stymied in the Plains states,

spinning your wheels, losing steam.
What began as whimsy—a tiny welt on the blue screen,
barely meriting a name—you blew a hole in town
after town, howling. You took on too much snow.

You became a hurricane. You slept over in New Orleans,
causing havoc, you rode into the Panhandle low and wet.
When will you cease this cycle of carnage and pain,
sleep soundly overnight, ease up on the hysterics?

When will you turn from tornado to rainbow,
from snowpocalypse to springtime?
We're tired of huddling against the wind in raincoats,
blowing into microphones, trying to track your erratics.

Lights Out

You are unprepared for the darkness, when it comes.
The one candle is always on a shelf you can't reach,
matches in a drawer somewhere you can't see.

Lights out. You were always afraid of what you'd find
in the dark, the monster in the closet, the bat in your hair.
But now, you suddenly notice the starlight, the eerie glow

coming from your laptop. You're afraid that the dark
won't hide you. You imagine yourself bathed in white light,
the UFO beam, the flashbulb, to calm your nerves.

Lights out. We rely on a power grid vulnerable
to EMP attacks, or just a storm or a hungry rat
chewing cables underground. We love our artificial

daytime. We've even forgotten how the full moon
used to feel, a brief chance to see into the dark,
a time of lunacy, of madness. Because it drove us mad

to have light outside of the sun. The thin filament of
incandescence, how it freed us but made work possible
after midnight. How it made us dependent, tired,

adding to our lonely hours. *Lights out, copper,*
the movie thugs used to say. It was not a good omen.
Time keeps getting away from us.

Lights out, your mother called through the echoing halls,
time for sleep. Now we seek the unfamiliar silence,
the strange solace of perfect dark.

Self-Portrait as Migration

Awkward on land, the loud honking and long necks,
snow geese gather en masse to meander in a muddy field,

belie the beautiful swirl of white as they move through
the November sky—as their bodies become a ghostly cloud

without beak or feet, nothing but white feathers suspended
in the air, like a magic trick. Trumpeter swans in a field

sparser, with black beaks and a different song altogether.
What happens in their flight over the snowy mountains?

Thousands may drop dead in a copper-contaminated lake.
Thousands more, confused, grow tired, stray off course.

In my body, cancer cells migrate from one terrain
to another, healthy cells taking flight, hemispheres

filling. I imagine my lymphocytes snow geese wings
inside me, a cacophony of sound and the rush and wonder—

which way will they fly? What will be left of me
after the white flash of their path has disappeared?

My Life Is an Accident

of DNA and radiation, a million missed chances
for death to sweep me off my feet.

Too much of this, not enough of that—
a witch's spell for trouble. Red-haired

and scarlet-fevered, born with wings and a tail,
an immune system weak as a kitten and a knack

for being in the wrong weeds at the wrong time.
Fascinated with systems, folders, and fossils,

tracking down each dinosaur and later, delivery systems
for rare anti-virals. Government research into nuclear facilities,

conspiracy theories linked to aliens and solar flares.
I was never meant, not planned, not absorbed into the mainstream,

never meant to survive this long according to charts and scans.
She's a miracle, they said, she's a mutant, she's a baby born

of a bad seed. Modern living makes a body bitter, our blood
and flesh filled with hormone disrupters, flame retardants and false

positives. But I'm a hay-maker, a harbinger,
a fateful warning of things to come.

Harbingers

Self-Portrait as Seismologist

I sleep with my ear to the ground,
listening for the signs of earthquake, tsunami,
the breakers of earth that move our surface.
Can you sympathize? She has endured meteors,
bombings, tree roots, wars and mass extinctions.
She keeps a dangerous history locked within layers.
Inside me, the uneasy swing of body waves
between fluid and solid measured, my shell cracking.
My teeth ache, bones vibrating. You wouldn't know
how listening to the earth shake each day fine-tunes
my ability to notice the faults, the unstable,
the fine lines between layers that lead to disruption,
eruption, smoke plumes, fires that spit into the sky.
Underneath it all—magnetic shifts, tidal waves,
plates disintegrating—we are all just barely holding it
together, the chaos rippling until we collapse.

I Can't Stop

Being a person who looks for the dark side.
Looking up crime statistics at Disneyland.
Looking for monsters under the bed.
Also, I can't stop taking pictures of flowers
even though mostly we have nine months of rain.
I can't stop wondering if the hummingbirds here
are doomed, if the snow geese will be poisoned
at an abandoned copper mine lake in Montana,
if that virus will reach us before we develop a vaccine.
So, I can't stop writing the apocalypse story over and over.
I've imagined the end before I'd even begun—
I wrote a nuclear winter poem when I was seven.
There was a boy in a symbolic green raincoat.
I watch football thinking of the boys with broken bones.
I watch wars thinking about people brought home
with missing limbs, nightmares, tremors.
I can't stop thinking about the jellyfish massing
in our warming ocean coast, the orca carrying her dead calf.
When I'm in the MRI tube, I can't help but think
of all the episodes of *X-Files* or *House* where people
had seizures within the MRI tube, for unexplained reasons.
Tonight I wonder if twenty-four years of marriage
are too many. I look at the picture of me at nineteen,
my eyes still hopeful but also afraid. I wonder when
someone I love will die. I wonder how many more holidays
I will celebrate. I told you, I can't stop introducing you
to so many clouds on my horizon. I'd rather tell you
about my nonstop love of Rainier cherries
or kissing in the rain. My nonstop love of even
old arcade games, the sound of them. I can't stop
thinking of the Doomsday Clock, how close we are
to spinning into the black hole at the center of our galaxy.

Reading Portents on the Summer Solstice

We wake up in Seattle shrouded in fog, darker than June
should be. Someone's called in another bomb threat.

That's how we'll remember this summer, a year
of shootings and trucks plowing into crowds, the tourists

running in terror on the television. The papers say the investigation
will continue. This morning you dropped a bottle of peppermint

oil, a shard of glass in the thick skin of your hand.
All around us, the sharp smell of mint follows.

The hummingbirds fight in the air over feeders and fuchsias,
the cool day finally grows sunny toward the end.

In high school the hot days went on forever, sticky until 10 PM,
lounging on the deck in the midwestern heat. What hothouse flowers

we were then, growing up too fast in the pressure of those June evenings.
Maybe we became explosive, unstable, unable to stay in one place too long.

Restless, we drove into the West, these unsunny persistent green shores
where we wait the rain out patiently. We've forgotten the insistent hum

that summer used to bring, the itch and swell of sunburn and bug bites.
We've let the cold creep into our insides. I've become allergic to the light.

Where I Come From

I was born from eggshell on a snow-covered beach.
I had my hair combed by palm fronds under sunny skies.

I grew up in a land of giant twisted apple trees
and radioactive wasps. Glowing swallows, white-tailed deer,

a land of verdant mutants. Tornadoes chased me to the edge.
I lived under bridges of wisteria branches, ivy, a carpet of damp flowers.

I escaped to a mountain, a tall forest of evergreens
older than us. They whispered their names to me,

they swallowed the songs of birds. Here I may hide away
forever in a tower of glass, guarded by sea-eagles,

the wind-blustered sky. Here no one may find me.
I blend in with the grey waves, the grey clouds let me finally rest.

Self-Portrait as Escape Artist

I could say at 42 I've escaped death already many times.
Maybe I was due, like a library book,
at an earlier age, but some spirit renewed me.

I almost drowned at three, then twice got scarlet fever
at 6 and 10. I could have died of my rare bleeding disorder
at 12; thanks to modern prescriptions, life prevailed.

I've become an expert at dodging tornadoes
and downed planes, traffic accidents and plain old bad luck.
I've been in a lot of hospitals where doctors made mistakes—

but still, woke up every time, little worse for wear.
I've been scared of death, but now he seems so familiar,
an old sweater I've casually tossed aside so often.

Please remember when I die that I was lucky
to be here at all—my mother's pregnancy uneasy,
my birth difficult and under an ill star, infancy involving

incubators for little baby blue me. So when I finally
take the fall, I must remember to say thank you
for the breaks that kept me ahead of the game so long.

I Thought You Can't Go Home Again

On this phone app they have you pick
your ideal calming backdrop
some of them are a tropical ocean
some of them snowdrops in space
none are my idea of calming
which if I recall was far into the woods
away from any sound at all
except maybe I remember cicadas
and the chittering of squirrels and the one mockingbird
that sounded like all the birds plus dogs barking
there were a lot of stray dogs in Tennessee
the way I was a stray
all of us were we ran around a lot away from grownup eyes
sometimes we got hurt and we bled
and got rocks embedded in our arms when we fell
but that doesn't stop me from remembering lying under the oak trees
and under the oak trees grew these miniscule violets
and tiny vibrant mosses so beautiful
they came and tore up my yard the trees the daffodils the strawberry patches
and they put down concrete and they left it like that for twenty years
just a lot of concrete where trees used to grow
five miles from Oak Ridge National Labs
and our neighbors with the farm their land was bought
and it's no longer a farmhouse
she had all these tiny figurines
and their house looked like *Little House on the Prairie*
They were old and had no children
like me and my husband will be someday
I don't own figurines but I have a lot of books
and no one to pass them on to
and I've finally got my own trees and grass
not enough to get lost in really
but I hope they don't turn it into concrete
one day you're in no-man's land rural country

the next it's a suburb and then a city
Some parts of the country are left to survive or not
like us as children, running around in the dark whooping it up
diving into ponds with forbidding signs saying "Not Safe"
just as unsure and unfrightened of our futures

Hospital Room, in April

After Sylvia Plath's "Tulips"

The white roses with frilled petals
brown beneath my fingertips, already.
Outside the air is blue, then grey, then night,
while in here the air is heavy, still,
always chilled by the fluorescent bulbs
that hum above us like insects.
Who is counting the hours
until the nurse comes back?
It is day, it is night, again.
All I want is water I can't keep down.
I keep a bottle of lavender oil
in my purse. I keep the bottle
open, a purifier for the air. Like lavender,
I am hardier than these flowers
in their vase. I will withstand
the days confined, unwatered,
without sunlight. Nutrients piped
in with needles. My stems tough
and hardened. My flowers almost
invisible, the tiny blooms explode,
cleanse and fill the room with blueness.

Mutant Sonnets: Self-Portrait as Bad 1950's Science Fiction Movie

The ones where aliens represent communists,
or robots represent nuclear destruction?
Would you be *The Giant Leech Woman* or *Killer Shrews?*
King Dinosaur or *The Night of the Giant Gila Monster?*
Always some monster coming in to wreck
the girls in bikinis dancing to bongo drums
on towels on the beach, in barns in the country,
the tinny radio stating "Be on the lookout..."
turned down just as it describes the oncoming atrocity.
Kids driving down an empty interstate too fast
encounter the wreckage—spacecraft, collapsed bridge,
burned bodies. What apocalypse, specifically,
is created from radioactive astronaut and mutant
dinosaur, can you face with square-jawed sheriff
at your side? Think hard before you point your pistol,
the laser gun, before you set the dynamite or A-bomb
on the life forms unique and pitiful, stranded
upon your planet, wishing only for home.

Supervillain, By the Sea, After the Summer of Bombs

September always makes me pensive.
This year, the headlines won't be grabbed
by any of my evildoings. I'm content to watch
the news seize the world by the throat with fear:
nuclear warheads, super volcanos, hurricanes, rafts of fire ants.
It's enough for me to recline and plan for tomorrow,
for a day when surely they will need me again
to shake things up and give the needed frisson.
Frankly, I've been uploading meditation apps,
trying out Pilates and holistic breathing.
Storing my superfoods, trying out new trends in grain bowls.
Watching a little Food Network before sleep.
Some of those guys look more like supervillains
than I do. I tried perfecting a gluten-free brownie recipe
and foreswore radioactive fish. When I think of the levels
I've already subjected myself to in my experiments,
well, let's just say I don't need any more Pacific tuna, thanks.
The waves lap cold at the edge of the world, the rocky lair
where I've been shoring up inspiration for a rainy day.
The light turns gold over the pine trees. For once,
I don't need to spoil anything.

Mutant Sonnets: Signs of Spring on the Way to More Medical Testing

Dawn viburnum and butter-bright forsythia
break through the weak March sun
as I lie down again before the machines
that read my insides, technicians passive
while my blood blooms with red and blue
flashes in the mushroom-grey of my heart,
as they inject bubbles in my veins,
while tumors traced in size and shape,
while lesions creep over the spongy layers of my brain.
What is blossoming? What is dying?
The birch tree sheds branches and the magnolia's
barely budding, and spring seems late, not enough warmth
in the wind yet to heat my skin, cold after scans.
Hard to find signs of rebirth here, in the cracks
of dead bark feeding woodpeckers, in the fragile petals
growing towards the sun, braving the blast of frost.

Grimoire

Have you tried the Wahl's protocol, asks one well-meaning friend,
kale, fish oil, blueberries? The Paleo diet or Ketogenic?

Our modern spells for ending illness, for mending brains
that have started to unravel. Exercise, vitamins, horse-whispering.

What are the words I whisper to myself over and over
at night in the hospital bed? The night nurse says I spoke

of murder, I was laughing. She could swear I was a witch,
with the essential oils of lavender and peppermint I brought

to exterminate the ghosts and medical smells,
to suffocate the scents of decay. I could share the prayers

and songs that bring me peace: Miyazaki's *My Neighbor Totoro*
and Disney's *Moana* on regular rotation as I learn again to walk

with a walker, as I struggle to hold a toothbrush. Be patient,
say the kind therapists who, like the earliest witches, know

the keys to healing include gentle hands, a smile for suffering,
sometimes, popsicles. I could use a little magic,

a few wise women. In my home my alchemies and elixirs await,
the familiar fur of my blue-eyed kitten, my husband's cooking

my first day home, potato soup the way my Irish mother liked it.
Here is the truth of it: the miracle, the secrets you seek

are already at work within me—the cells that strive
for homeostasis, for regeneration, for immortality.

In the Time Between Sunspots

We learned more about our own footprint,
the shape of our bodies in space, the crowding out
of certain species. We studied the fossil record.

During this solar minimum, we felt hot, fretted.
The magnetic poles were changing.
The hummingbirds left, confused, for the mountains.

We learned about love from old musicals.
We rejected sleight of hand. We noticed
the butterflies' flight paths. We grew lettuces.

We planned an escape path and built palaces
on the edge of the earth. We loved staring
at the horizon, the long blue stretch between.

In the end we felt the corners closing in.
We started fighting among ourselves.
We hoarded apples and bullets.

We forgot that there would be another cycle,
that this was not the end, just an ending.
We learned to dance inside circles of light.

Flare

Solar flares eject plasma beyond the sun's corona,
radiation emitted by solar flares may disrupt radar, radio.

Its mechanisms are not well understood.

My first flare came on the week of the solar eclipse
when the shadow fell cold over us, and the birds stopped singing.

I wasn't ready to loosen my grip, to lose my footing.
I wasn't ready to lose to multiple sclerosis.

Rosa "sun flare" produces yellow blooms in my garden.
In 2012 a massive solar storm barely missed earth.

We are waiting for the next. We cannot predict,
its mechanisms are not well understood.

A girl, bright blonde, stands with the sun behind her—
tendrils escape the corona of her hair.

My flare lit up the MRI, white coronas around black holes.
I fell down a lot. I couldn't speak. I couldn't remember names.

There is a web site, solarweather.com. It records
flare sprays, lists solar storms, makes predictions, but

the light made me dizzy. The air was filled with smoke.
I felt at any time I could fall off the edge of the earth. Tilting.

My mechanisms are not well understood.

Someday our sun may flame out in a superflare
like other stars around the universe,

like me, waiting for the light-up of neural networks,
waiting for it to burn me up, waiting to become

a flicker of brightness in the dark.

Self-Portrait as Desert During a Superbloom

Just waiting beneath my skin during the dry months,
dry years: brittlebrush and primrose, desert lily and lupine,
their fierce color against the fire-tinged morning sky.
These flowers are a metaphor for something:
sleeping ghosts or memories or dreams of hues
I had lost, kept hidden for years.
Suddenly the landscape isn't sand but pink blossom,
lush with birdsong of grackles on cacti,
roadrunners leaving little triangle tracks
in the dust. I'm so prolific you can see me from space,
a yellow ribbon. I want the burst and bloom,
a carpet of wildflowers that evaporate.

The jackrabbit and quail scrabble in my shadow.
I'm a hot wind in your lungs.
I'm the sun and the bold blue sky overhead,
the spiked shadows' silhouettes in afternoon,
when the petals close against the bright heat,
the cold sharp stars at night.
Watch out for snakes underfoot, javelinas, scorpions
in the suddenly pastel underbrush. I've had enough
drear and bleak and blurred images to last a lifetime,
enough tumbleweed and drought. I am a cactus flower,
a sand verbena, sunflower. I am ephemeral.
Catch me before I wilt and fade beneath your gaze.

One More Attempt at Disaster Preparedness

Because it's got to be more than water bottles and batteries,
an escape plan and a full tank of gas.
It's also what to do when you get the diagnosis you might not survive,
when your legs give out unexpectedly beneath you,
when your organs flutter and fail one by one.
Will you know what the fight or flight will even involve?
How many nights have you already spent in ICUs, how many
in emergency rooms—could you map them out, like fireflies
on a path? If you needed help with—talking, say, or breathing,
what would be your secret weapon? I've got a chest full
of medicines that may or may not do me any good.
While you watch the flu map take down children, despite vaccines,
beneficial bacteria missing or altered gene misstep—
or three hurricanes at once bear down on your coast,
or wildfires near your hospital, your neighborhood—
all disasters become less abstract, more personal.
A friend that visits with no warning, a song lyric you remember
vaguely from junior high. You may or may not survive
no matter how prepared you are—the stardust that whirls around us,
the solar flares that interrupt our radio waves, one body more or less
making such a small impact. Your own little sun dimming,
your horizon, tipping towards darkness, disappears.

Some Nerve: A Nocturne

Tonight my nerves are frayed wires
alerting me to the full Strawberry Moon

out my window. The coyotes
yip. They sound like girls shrieking.

There are birds hammering
against the dead trees inside my head.

Against my skin the nerves alert
to pain, to cold, to heat, to touch.

I shake in my sleep. I'm going to pieces,
I tell my doctor. We trace the processes

tangled from brain to spine. If I can pinpoint
on my body the messages, maybe I can

interrupt them. Maybe I'll start wearing
a tinfoil hat, like that man told me.

Maybe it's the aliens after all,
wired into my teeth. Anyway, I'm jittery.

I'm not really sleeping. Inside my skull,
electricity flares. The voltage keeps going up.

Nightmares. Trembling. I'll tell you now,
my nerves are bad tonight.

Broken chords in the nocturne. Frayed.
The sparks kicking up. The coyotes crying.

The moon hums in its rosy halo,
an atmosphere of radioactive dust.

Meltdown

I won't deny I'm fragile. There's been incidental damage in transit. Who will sign? It was raining Cesium-138 the morning I was born. It was in the green apples I ate in the garden. I've secreted away iodinc-131 in my organs. I've listened to the clicking of the dosimeter. I learned how to use a Geiger counter to measure snow as a child. I grew green and fragrant, tumors in my liver and thyroid, blood and bone corrupted, uncontrolled. Like the boars, deer, the wolves that escape government detection, like the hot wasps, swallows, and catfish, I will build a home somewhere you'd never expect, ticking away until meltdown. You can house me in concrete, silver, cadmium towers. Like a fairy tale, there are terrors underground, women motionless in coffins, babies wailing without mothers, ready and waiting to inflict judgment, a dull green flame on the horizon.

Self-Portrait as February Morning

Stormy and oppressively dark. The birds
flutter where the tree branches should have leaves out
by now. The daffodils refuse to budge.

You know in theory spring is coming,
nearly around the corner, but for now,
the cold bites at your fingertips, your face.

The deer have eaten the bottom branches
and bark off all the trees. They look despondent.
There is never enough hot coffee. It's hard—

the grey of the sky, the threat of snow and ice,
the frost on the grass, and waking up alone seems
an impossible quest. No one loves February,

its emptiness, the dourness of Lent and saccharine
of St. Valentine, a month so short but so long,
of heavy sweaters, flimsy scarves and wet socks.

Oh, to wake up April, away from this bluster,
to open the door to blossom and sun,
instead of this bitter, too-thin light.

Cancer Scare

It will happen on a sunny day when other things
are happening that are more important—
the lilacs will bloom, or the moon will stand out full and lovely.
It will be an incidental finding on a scan they did "just to be safe."
It will mean writing a will, thinking about who you want
handling your things, your spouse, after you are gone.
I don't know what yours will look like—
mine was a minefield of jelly beans, quail egg-sized
tumors, thriving somewhere inside my body,
a minefield waiting for a misstep.
Where is cancer born? Cancer is part of us.
From our own cells, healthy, then, striving to be immortal—
tiny monsters unwilling to give up or go home.
Cancer is an arsonist, setting fire to your plans, your future.
Cancer is a zombie army within, a ravenous horde.
For you, will the sun set with a happy ending,
a benign cyst removed and a clean bill of health?
Or will it be the surprise twist, with an uncertain lingering
over the tiniest details—the way a strawberry tastes,
the sun on your skin, the bright obscene burst
of pink on the azaleas—then, fade to black,
beep, beep, breathe, say goodnight.

Self-Portrait as Wisteria on a May Night

Your blossoming turns the night purple and fizzy, like grape soda.
The bees are drunk on it. Underneath your blooms
the heavy burden of settling and resettling, a flower that moves in
and takes over, threatening wooden beams, toppling towers.
Called poisonous and invasive merely for being successful
and after all, you feed the butterflies, take root
in poor soil and all kinds of weather.
You are a winner, wisteria. You came here alone,
an immigrant, a stranger, and flourished.
Anyone who doesn't understand can walk beneath
your twisting vines in spring, early in the evening
when the sun starts to mellow, breathe the sweet heavy air,
touch the trusting tails of your petals. You're so beautiful,
it will never matter what you strangle,
what weaker-willed plant stood in your path and perished.

Introduction to Writer's Block

It was right after they had taken a picture of my brain and showed me those dark shadows, called lesions. You said *You've lost your muse* and you took me to the movies, to museums, we walked along the ocean and in the mountains, and still I couldn't write. *I've lost my words* I told you, although technically we knew they were still in there, somewhere, teeming and crowding, but sometimes I would confuse one with another, another aphasia. You can write with just the words you have left, I told myself. *Writers write*, so you just sit down and do it. What stories are left to tell? My brain has been crammed full of riots and police beatings, bombings in distant lands that were the birthplaces of roses and pomegranates and apples, salmonella in the peanut butter, sunspots causing continental drift. You have to shove all that aside. Maybe listen to some music, that new band, something with dragons. Even at the end of the world, you can make fire. If you wait long enough, something inside you will ignite.

Self-Portrait as Mutant

We fear the fidgeting of GMOs, spider DNA in the corn,
crab DNA in the goat milk. But one by one our genes

are ticking off and on, dazzling but broken Christmas lights,
deciding on green eyes for this baby, an extra rib for that one.

Magic powers are a maybe. For me, born with mutations
you might not see, passing for normal, even—knowing any offspring

might be in danger, might carry away the swirl of misspent organs—
I must make the decision, join the gene pool
or not. I am one of God's fearfully and wonderfully made,

emphasis on fearfully, miscreant and misstep, heat and fury,
blood and bone. Too many ticked off species. One more mistake.

Chaos theory makes beauty of a mess.
When I was little I looked more like you.

This is evolution, fractal-turned-screen-saver, mistakes turned
magic, one more leap into the chasm of natural selection.

April In Middle Age

I find myself not asking *am I still sexy*
like all the magazines seem to demand
but *am I happy am I falling apart*
Part of us decaying part of us radiant
There's a balance on the whole
as our eyeballs thicken it corrects
so many stigmatisms and while I might be dead
I'm not
so that's a celebration
worthy of pink cake and streamers
and right now there are cherry blossoms
tulips a whirl of petals in the air making all
the little indignities of aging (organs betraying us
growing tumors teeth falling out spine compressed
DNA unraveling cells loosening their grip without warning)
seem worth it as long as I can still taste cherry popsicles
and remember how Coke was before it was new
before internets and smartphones and apps
we had music on scratched plates
we had long boring stretches of summertime
we did not have helicopter parenting
we had bikes without helmets wind in our faces
we had exploration of caves without grownups
and now I am a grownup I still like to explore
will continue to put my face in the flowers
grab at handfuls of grass and dirt in April
I will put on a dress with roses and lipstick
and somehow regenerate
a cyborg of space and spring.

Self-Portrait as a Body Shaped by Illness

My brain forms storm clouds.
My veins run hot and cold.
The idea of weather passes through
my joints, fingers, spine,
tingling with the rain.
Fire burns in the passes,
smoke in my hair. My nails
glitter like lightning. My limbs
are loosened, serpents that refuse to stay still,
my lips too twisted to kiss.
My throat a knotted root.
My two feet untethered, able to float,
tipped to tangle. Take me in your arms,
I will not remain the same—
first one form, then another:
a tree, a lake, a swan, a changeling
that burns its image into the bed.

Blood Moon

Self-Portrait as Flare

The moon is as dark as blood and ash is falling from the sky.
Around us the mountains are on fire.
Inside me a flare is robbing me of memory,
my legs' strength, my sense of balance. My mouth
forgetting how to form certain words the way
our beloved rain has abandoned us.
They talk risk management:
putting me in a wheelchair, building in
adaptive structures—a future of ramps and bars.
Like me, our city balances on a ring of fire,
a nest of volcanoes and fissures in our edge
of the continent. Our bodies' betrayals
like teens in a dry forest tossing fireworks
as they walk, destroying worlds on a whim.
We are all fragile and ready for sudden instabilities,
for our structures to go up in flames, forgotten.
We etch our stories into architectures of stone and paper,
knowing we must hurry before the inflammation consumes it all.

Every Time I Take Another Cancer Test, I Feel the Universe Collapsing

In on me like the special effects of a cheesy movie about dreams
or time travel, the walls of reality tilting in on themselves like glass panes

as doctors discuss tumor markers, scans and measurements in monotone.
Is this an MRI tube or perhaps an isolation chamber on a trip to Mars

because life has become scary like bad sci-fi, in fact I expect a villain
with a microscope and supergerms to jump out at any moment.

I would like to ignore any ignoble cells gone awry, avoid the needles
and radioactive machines, almost like avoiding the ending

of the story. I don't want to read the last page just yet, no spoilers,
I want the party scene with the band and the unicorns to keep going,

a magical garden opening up before me, each path eternal and symmetrical
each footfall silent on grass that provides a green escape, a patient place to fall.

Under a Blood Moon, I Get My Brain Scanned

Between large magnets. A coyote crossed our path
on the way to the hospital, low to the ground.
The moon is red and menacing, the air

claustrophobic. The ER doctor hands me a diagnosis:
multiple sclerosis, probably there for years.
I try not to make a catastrophe movie

in my head. Instead of white matter lesions,
I picture dinosaurs and dragons, my brain fighting
to stay out of wheelchairs, out of the hospital,

to keep my hands and feet and mouth working,
to keep writing, my chain link fence of
neural sparks fizzling away. This is not the end,

though it may feel like one type of ending.
A bad moon rising. A diagnosis. A degree of uncertainty.
The small rabbits nibbling at the leaves of my dahlia,

leaving the stems dangling, ravaged,
just as these marks make my brain less whole,
full of holes, holy. The lights not quite extinguished.

July, in the Garden, I Feel like Death

Last year at this time the doctors shook their heads.
I felt fine. They said I had six months, max. Nothing
they could do. Radiation, blah, chemo, blah.

This week I felt like dying but it was really only
multiple sclerosis. The doctors beamed at me for my great act
of surprise and heroism—not dying. They patted my hand.

I have been spending time trying to make my little
plot of land better. Lavender I planted last fall,
when I still thought I might not see spring,

roses coaxed into blooming, rampant sweet peas.
I water and snip and watch them, benevolent
as the sun. I cannot seem to keep my own body

tidy as my garden, which is not that tidy, not compared
to my neighbors, retired ladies with roses trained up trellises
and whole armies of spectacular clematis, honeysuckle.

I wish I could tame this garden inside me, this wayward
biome that taxes even the most careful caretaker.
I will plant myself here in sandy soil, under sunny skies.

Self-Portrait as Late August Evening

I will be gone soon, and with me, summer.
These warm breezes fleeting; the beauty I have
is the beauty of all things that disappear
before you know you'll miss them.
Each mood—sultry and scorching, mild and balmy—
changeable as the rise of the moon's face,
one moment blue over corn fields, another
orange over the tree tops, or red dropping over the sea.
No one loves August—we all long for September,
her sweater sets and the chill of her rain—
though the end always comes, an unwelcome surprise.
Through the still air, the wings of birds rustle the dry grass.
I am waiting, heavy as the apple tree branches weighted down
with uneaten apples, turning the air sweet and rotten.

That Summer

I woke to the smell of smoke.
Sunset was red haze.
The rain was on a holding pattern, just off the horizon.
Our conversations were short,
we tried not to breathe too deeply.
We gathered herbs that purified.
We dreamed of ice.
Under the mountains,
the earth tried to shake us off.
The oldest oak trees fell,
people sheltered and burned in swimming pools,
the screams of horses in the air.
My brain couldn't connect—my legs
trembled, my speech slurred. You took me to the hospital,
they tried to tether me with IVs.
I was tied to a troubled body.
We were tied to a troubled earth.
You said it was too late to leave anyway.

Self-Portrait as MRI

You think you know me because you've seen a map
to my brain? There's nothing there but the stars,
the constellations of glowing debris
of a war of nerves: damage, inflame, attack.

The face-cage, the thumping echo chamber
coffin-tube, nothing romantic about this enforced
stillness, this live burial. The invisible magnet's fingers
deciding: this brain this joint this blood this scar this bone.

They say you can see the consciousness
of the comatose in these maps,
the God-spot where the divine resides
inside us. I don't know if I believe

in these science fictions, these certainties
of soul. Where is the piece of me
smiling in a field of red tulips, back
when I was still me, before the explosions

started making inroads. What about our faces
pressed together at a pumpkin farm, the blazing
orange, the cheesy scarecrow, catching the late autumn
sunshine? Where are those tucked away

in the scan before you, the mind's obvious circuits
malformed and malfunctioning? My self-portrait
lies outside these discernible outlines, these false
atlases to what lasts inside of us.

Unnerved

To fluster, to agitate. When my eyelids flutter,
my iris starts shaking, the vertigo tips me over—
yes, you would be discomfited, I think,
if the damage to neurons brings on
crying fits and finger twitching,
legs that suddenly sink underneath or
feet that miss the mark on the path.
You too would be rattled, discombobulated,
if suddenly your vision blackened,
your memory blanked on the last two minutes.
Your brain and spine no longer reliable,
spitefully throwing obstacles between you
and simple things: walking, throwing a ball,
typing a page. To psych out, to unsettle,
to needle. Yes, to enfeeble. These are all
the right terms for this. I've come undone,
unglued, unnerved, an earthquake mapped
out inside my mind, volcanic anomalies underneath,
an instability, an unhinged person, no longer
safe on the wobbling ladder of perception,
path and vision no longer true or trustworthy.

Blood Moon, Flare, Coyote

The blood moon was heavy
in the sky. A coyote darted in front
of us in the car on the way to the hospital.
I learned this disaster was named "flare,"
like a solar flare, blazing in the brain,
creating bright halos of inflamed nerves,
causing messages to darken, flame out—
legs, vision, uncertain hands fumbling,
dizzy, ready to fall. Like the moon itself
was falling out of the sky there, not set
among the stars but jarred, uncertain.
It has betrayed us, no longer a bright beacon
but a prophesy where the moon is dark as blood,
a witch's sign, a bad omen, a magic
you cannot hold safely within you.

How to Survive

The zombie apocalypse: Be lucky. Be prepared. Be skilled in the industrial arts, or maybe martial arts. Sneak in swords. Swallow antibiotics. Don't trust your neighbor. Don't bring a baby. Don't forget the double-tap.

A fire: Be light on your feet. Be light for carrying. Bounce off the sides of the building, bounce off the fireman's tarp, bounce out the open window into the waiting arms.

A plague: Be an outlier. Be a mutant, genes ready to absorb new knowledge, new reactions, new antibodies. Be alone, in the desert or the snow, places germs cannot survive, or people. Your cells must be slayers, ready for the attack.

A tsunami: Stop collecting seashells. Be uphill. You cannot outrun, sometimes with its speed water overtakes cars in their desperate hurry. Do not look back, do not carry baggage or a small child on your back, be sure you climb upwards, upwards, leaving the swirling black debris at your feet.

Drowning: Be airy. Train your lungs to hold tight. Be a mermaid. Be a seal. Grow gills and speak to fish to show you their secrets.

The truth is, there is no final secret, there is no formula to save us. To survive is simple: to wake up, open our eyes, take a single breath.

Don't forget to pack your pockets. Don't forget your masks and moguls, whatever your weapons might be. Sing your song, put the note in a bottle, be remembered, because someday soon, we will all be gone.

The Year I Was Dying

Was pretty tough. I went through all the phases:
denial, anger, ice cream, mortgage-signing,
with equal aplomb. I ignored all the evidence
against me. I took vitamins and drank juices

in the hopes of some last-minute salvation.
I believed in miracles. They were in the air
that summer, along with the angst and wildfire fumes.
Every minute I carried a camera. I watched

every second of Seattle spring with an aching
sense of loss. Pink blossoms, falling, sakura zensen,
that acute sadness of beauty that disappears.
The moon too appeared in a lot of pictures.

I sheltered a kitten all blue eyes and white fluff
and named her Sylvia. I avoided her namesake's poetry,
though, her obsession with death the opposite
of what I wanted. She didn't understand.

I took a lot of slow walks with my husband,
just where we wanted to go—by that waterfall
in the woods, on the cold ocean banks
where sometimes we'd see otters.

I spent money on things, like I would continue.
I made a funeral playlist, mostly vaguely folkish.
I prayed but often forgot to bargain.
I exercised and made myself as strong

as I could. I tried not to say the word "cancer"
to my friends at parties. I did not think
about the tumors in my liver, except to wish
them to shrink, to disappear like those spring flowers,

crumpling in the bright sun, turning to dust.
How could they get to me, here,
while I was taking these photos,
proving every second that I was here,

that my eyes were on these trees, this man,
this moon, all mine, all of them, this minute.

Self-Portrait as Stranger

Little girls are taught to fear strangers,
especially talking wolves, especially on the trail
to grandmother's house,
but sometimes, as in old westerns,
a Stranger is a savior,
an angel, a one-person army of God.
What these towns are like after the stranger
leaves is up for grabs. "Come back, Shane,"
echoes a little boy's voice. But Shane won't
be back. A Stranger Comes to Town,
it has been said, is one of two plots.
But could I be that stranger? The steely
eyes, the mysterious past, the way
I walk with a limp? Used to be a
gunslinger, a gambler, an outlaw, a sniper.
Who knows? Their past is dimly lit.
Did I tell you I was related to Jesse James?
And how I used to be a really good shot?
But these days I'm only good for a few things:
planting trees, poems, looking after animals
in the woods. Did I mention I was going
to grandmother's house? Did I tell you
why I wear a red cloak? I know
the rest of the story. The Stranger
brings rage, deliverance, hope.
They ride on a pale horse.
This time, I will bring vengeance.

Mutant Sonnets: Full Cold Wolf Moon, Winter Solstice

This moon shines on the longest night of the year.
The coyotes are yipping into the darkness.
Tonight I am tearing paper, tossing it into the flames.
Tonight I will dream of a new body, as bright and strong
as the moon with its shivering cover of frost.
My cherry tree foolishly puts out blossoms.
It's a night for wolves and snow queens in sleds.
It's a night where we bravely face the sunset, even so.
Light up a tree, put flowers in a vase, roast something
in an oven. Sometimes the full moon makes me uneasy,
sleepless. Sometimes the wide wake of winter
shakes me. Who knows what waits for us as the days
grow longer? The fire crackles. Inside I know something kindles.

In the Movie of My Life

I'm a mutant girl growing up in an atomic playground,
playing tag with the children of nuclear physicists.

I talk to foxes in a magical, toxic forest.
As I grow older, I learn to hide myself

from malevolent thorns, radioactive waste, all the dangers
until boy meets girl. There is a love story. I flee the castle

to start my own glass kingdom by the sea.
Years of marriage don't damage our DNA.

He learns to cook gluten-free blueberry crumb cake.
I dream of turning into swans, dragons, into ravens and hummingbirds.

In my dreams I always have wings. I become a poet.
The end, of course, is appropriately tragic. I end up pale

somewhere by the ocean, whispering goodbye.
He mourns my loss by playing eighties alternative music

against a montage of photographs of us laughing together.
He plants fields of mutated flowers in my memory.

I Am Not Expecting

A boy. Or a girl. Don't worry. Don't arrange
any showers, buy me any presents, pink or blue.
I will never be expecting. So no balloons or blankies,
no pregnancy rumors, no "will they or won't they."
The doctors told me "No" at an early age.
So my husband and I grow older, with no children,
just a garden and a string of cats. It's not bad news because

I am not expecting to die, even though
doctors told me I would be dead in six months
a while ago. I mean, I will die someday
but not this year. Not from cancer.
The tumors have been labeled
"If not benign, at least indolent."
That is the good news you receive
about tumors. I was not expecting

to receive a diagnosis of multiple sclerosis
after 40 years on this earth. Sure,
I was clumsy, sure I had tremors,
I had fallen, I had broken bones,
I was forgetful. But I could not foretell
the damage in my brain, white matter lesions,

a pattern the doctors could put a name on.
Congratulations! It's MS! No cards for that.
No flowers. A nasty sort of surprise.
Trips to the hospitals for scans and steroids.
Nothing romantic or wondrous. No cause
for celebration. Except: I am still here,
and I am not expected to be elsewhere

for a while. So today I will take a walk
under wisteria, and watch the hummingbirds.
I will read and listen to music while I still can.
I am not expecting much more
out of this life. Just a few more days,
a few more hours to stare out at the blue sky,
to plant one more tree, to write this poem,
to tell you: don't worry, I'm not expecting much.

Sitting by Yourself at the End of the World—I Mean, Year

You start to wonder about the luck
in the bottom of the bowl: noodles, black-eyed peas, grapes.

After the disappointments, the almost-ends, a year insistent
on driving itself in the murky light of December, a drunken

swerve into death's waiting arms, what can we expect from tomorrow?
Here's my hope: for health, for penguin families,

for quiet long days of sunshine. Once more, with feeling.
can we celebrate with fireworks the explosions of ambition

and anger, an America that may be disintegrating before our eyes,
children who've forgotten anything but the touchscreen and LED?

In the grey fog, it may be the bangs and whimpers will go unnoticed.
The fragments forgotten, the torn limbs buried, unseen.

This year I was told I had six months to live, and now it's been seven.
Buying time is all I can hope for. It seems now's the time to put on the sparkly

dress, stand in line to see the stars, make the leap unimagined.
Each grape for a lucky month, each pop a promise.

Corona

2020 Didn't Start

Out the way we'd hoped. We had the rainiest January on record.
My grandfather died. I had my first root canal.

Also, impeachment. Then volcanos, earthquakes, coronavirus.
Who wouldn't be curled up eating Oreos in bed at this point

in the year? I know: we put on running shoes, we run up our credit cards,
we stay on the run so we can't hear the pounding of the world in our ears.

I played eighties music because I remember when the world wasn't so bad,
or at least, we didn't think it was, and all kids wanted to go to Space Camp.

We dreamed of rocket ships. There wasn't so much direct comparison to Hitler.
I couldn't hear the screams reverberating on Twitter.

Today I forgot to do my hair and drank margaritas instead. I didn't pay
my bills and planted primroses all around the perimeter.

Doesn't it feel a bit apocalyptic in here? Maybe we should buy those filtrating
face masks and tend to the fire. Watch the shadows as the flames blaze higher,

listen to the coyote howl solitary in the cold winter nighttime.
We're whisper-close to midnight. Tick tock.

Wish You Were Here (Postcard from a Pandemic)

We talked yesterday about how
it might be the last time
we saw each other, what did we say then?
How I said I wasn't scared

but I was. It's different here
on this side of the water—more deaths,
the statistics seem louder. I hope
you are trying to garden.

I sent you a letter and some Tylenol.
You still have my sweater and my circular saw.
The last time we ate dinner together,
we should have said a prayer.

We should have said goodbye.
Here is a picture of you from 12th grade.
I will remember you, when all else has perished.
I will remember you when humanity has been erased

from the earth, when we have become
fairy tales, like dragons, faintly remembered.
You will be flying and carrying a sword.
I will be wearing a red cloak, surrounded by fire.

A Conspiracy of Ravens Began

Do you remember the night before you died,
the way the moon was a silver sliver,

the wind pushed the dead leaves along the ground?
And the ravens, those corvids, sat outside my window,

the way their dark wings foreshadowed everything.
The smell was of something burning, chemical

and acrid. I used to sing songs about flying
away. I used to be a believer. Do you remember

that? I used to be bright as a flower.
The night you died, what did you used to say to me,

that you loved my nose, that you'd follow me anywhere?
And now I cannot follow. It's so dark

I cannot follow the shadows outside my window.
The moon is almost nothing. Do you remember

the last thing you said, the way the ravens
outside were screaming your name,

the way the whole earth shook beneath us,
the way the night arrived as if it would never end?

When It All Falls Apart

You can clutch at the remnants with your fingers,
you can breathe and meditate, you can rant and rave.
You can hold the hands of those closest and pray.

What will you take as the city burns, as the volcano erupts,
when your landscape is cinders and ash?
Will you have the strength to hold it all together,

when the atoms, the bees, the planets—all trying to fly apart?
In the storm of zombie apocalypse, or in the quiet of a waiting room
who are you willing to save, or lose? Are you ready

to face the coming dark? We all teeter at the end, unsure of our next
steps, what awaits, a bright light or dark grave, a final blow,
the way we look at the birthday candles and say, "Make a wish."

May dragons or angels await you. May your memory burn like an imploding star.

To Survive So Many Disasters

You wonder: are you cursed?
If you are a curse.
Your high school torn apart by tornadoes,
homes destroyed by fire and earthquake and flood,
though you always narrowly escape.
What narrative are you writing in which
you are the sole survivor?
Cities crumbling, you don't look back
lest you are turned to salt.
You were warned. You promised
never to return. You set out on a journey
far from home. You looked out into darkness
and saw possibility. Well now, read your own palm—
even with that splintered lifeline, how many times
is it possible to escape death?
Once, twice, three times? Nine? The doctors cursed you
since the day you were born blue—
scarlet fever, drowning, cancer, or bleeding?
Your brain slowly decaying?
They are always telling you
when to die, but you ignore them,
tripping along with your basket.
All the leaves sharp-edged in the moonlight.
Your grandmother will tell you she was the wolf all along.
You know she's right. You take up the hood
and once again walk the trail towards a new city,
even knowing your footsteps doom us all.

This Is the Darkest Timeline

One that started with a roll of the dice,
an election gone awry, a time of fire and flood.
When we started to panic at every pandemic,
went into quarantine playing quarters.

We've all become the evil versions of ourselves
just trying to get back to the prime timeline,
the one where everything went right,
when our memories weren't clouded by calamity.

That butterfly that flapped its wings,
the animal virus gone rogue. We couldn't buy
butter or bullets. We waited with bated breath
underground. When we emerge anew

it will be with new eyes, our currency
changed from cash to cashews and cheese
sandwiches. You can't remember the taste
of food without tin. You can't remember

how to kiss. Your sense of time scrambled.
You learned to throw a knife and gut fish.
The darkest timeline has taken us
the way of apocalypse, earthquake,

super volcanoes, and tidal waves.
We can't take any more disaster.
We've buried too many bodies
and sheltered in place too long to forget.

When we started this journey it was
"nothing left to lose," now we're too tired
to remember how fresh fruit used to smell,
the pale pink of cherry blossoms,
the days before the coyotes took over our streets.

When I Said Goodbye

I didn't know it would be like this,
the cold and the very stillness of it.

I always mistook enemies for friends, lovers
for eternity. And now a crumpled dress,

some dead flowers in a book. It's all so
melodramatic. I apologize. I never liked opera,

preferred Nick Drake, Cat Stevens. You know,
all that music where you drift down a river,

your hair spread out like Ophelia, holding a crown
in your hands as you turn cold.

I always believed the lies, that's my fault.
They told me it would be okay,

and I thought that meant something. Happy endings
aren't so easy to find, not in history, not even the storybooks.

So, play me a last song. Promise me something,
that you won't forget those very small moments,

when we fell asleep with the white cat on our pillow,
the first ice cream in Paris, daffodils in Tennessee,

the butterfly on my hand in that beam of sunlight in the woods,
the way I ran through the grass, laughing.

Don't remember me like this, grim-faced, after all the bad decisions.
Don't remember the war. Just remember the sweetness,

how it was once. Leave me covered in clichés and lilacs.

February 2020 and It's Time

for another apocalypse. This time
it's pandemics, or is it asteroids?
It all seems like an eighties novel
by Stephen King I read in junior high.
I was not very optimistic as a kid,
I saw the world through *Silent Spring* glasses,
everything tinted with nuclear fallout.
We will probably be fine. This coronavirus
is beautiful, a circle with a glowing crown, a halo.
An angelic killer. After all, it's just trying
to survive. Just like us. We must make space
for bluebirds and viruses alike, for falling stars
and near-miss meteors. We watch the sky
for a sign. We read horoscopes that tell
us when we should open up in our relationships
or wish on lucky numbers. We believe
in too much. Anyone watching the February
sky, the way it shakes the dead branches and
resists any weather prognostications,
you should know—well, life is unpredictable.
You cannot count on things. We count
too much. We use our calculators and our AI
and satellites and we miss all the tiny factors
that will be our doom—one little coronavirus,
one little rock in space—just one too many
and our careful structures collapse. Don't trust
the almanacs, the ancient stones. Don't read the tea leaves.
Let's go out the way we've always dreamed,
hair down, dancing in the flames, arms raised to the sky.

Planting Camellias as Act of Resistance

Bright March morning after snow.
News headlines about rising sea lines,
starving orcas, droughts. Early spring
brings bomb cyclones. Everyone
at the top's a criminal. Cesium in the
sunflowers, strontium-90 in the dust.
This morning I dig in the dirt and plant
flowers, unnecessary, flagrant: a pink
camellia, jonquils, primroses. The blue jays
a tinnitus in the air, the little juncos jittering.
The resistance a wall of flowers rising
against the poison, against the screaming,
the satellites, wars and newsrooms. I don't like
feeling helpless, silent in the face
of so much terror, so today I make plum jam.
The doctors say my nerves are getting thinner.
No wonder, shrinking against the agitation, atoms
vibrating together with the supermoon.
My brain has blank spaces now,
illumined by inflammation.
They say we will bring change, the moon
and me. Listen: every breath in this air
is an amplification, every petal a protest.

Tick. Tick. Boom.

You should have listened to that voice
in your head, the one that told you
to get the hell out of town, get out
to a cabin in the woods and stay there.

You saw that 2016 was a year of failure,
but what you didn't see coming
could be a major motion picture.
You watched the virus cross China,

seep over borders. Viruses do not
follow orders. You should have been
smarter. You should have bought
more bleach and paper towels, checked out

more library books. You've always been
good at the moment before the crash,
the feeling before the neighbor burned
his house down, and the moment after:

the strawberries growing in the charred wreckage.
Could you have altered history if only
you'd tried a little harder, rung the alarm bell
a little louder? No one was listening at Christmas.

As a child, you could hear the tick of the Geiger counter,
the click on the phone line. Your whole life
you've been primed for disaster. You read
Greek mythology and the Foxfire Books.

Cassandra's story so much sadder because she knew
what was coming. You've been tracing the fissures
with your fingers on the map. You've stockpiled
water. You still couldn't see what was right in front of you.

Listen. The tick in your head.
The flowers bloom, bloom. Boom.
Countdown to midnight. Will you be found wanting?
They'll never catch you now.

In a Plague Year, I Held a Glass Baby

During the plague year, I plant so many things:
walls of herbs, extravagant dahlias, a hummingbird garden.

Without any touch at all, an immaculate conception:
a glass baby grows inside me. All the scans attest.

A miracle child, delicate as sugar or snow.
It's not your imagination. It's not God visiting

you, not your Magnificat. It's just, you had time
on your hands and so much energy. You planted

so much a flower bloomed inside you.
It could have been a tumor, a shadow, a misread.

At any rate, I hope by the end of the Plague Year
I will give birth to a magic baby, one so fragile

she cannot be touched. She'll glisten in the sunlight.
She deserves a castle surrounded by a high rose bramble.

In a Plague Year, we are all having babies. We sing them
songs in the night to quiet their voices.

You see, my baby may be imaginary. All the ultrasounds
come back inconclusive. I wrap myself in eyelash sweaters

and fuzzy pink blankets. You never know what the end
of a plague will bring. First the bloom of spring,

then death, or angels, or a chrysalis baby, born
in a peach, bamboo shoot or a sweetpea, a magic blessing,

a baby that rides a butterfly and sips from a thimble.
The end won't be so hard, now. The shuttering of light,

the long cold nights. Remember I've been planted.
Planting. Planed. All that's left is a miracle.

Serendipity

You write your fortune on a five-dollar bill and hand it to the attendant.
The five-dollar bill passes through many hands. They all inherit your fortune.

I believed in magic for long enough that magic became part mindset. I could speak with animals at the zoo, I could protect people I loved from death. I conveyed blessings to baby rabbits.

Live long enough and you injure yourself, become unsteady, unstable.
Take time to enjoy the flight, the run through the new grass, that first strawberry.
Because someday, it all will.

Once upon a time a princess. A dragon. Once upon a time you were born, you were loved and blessed, then stolen by a witch. Once you slew the dragon and were sad. You wore armor and carried a shining sword. There was a happy ending, or an unhappy one, depending on the version you discovered.

What can I tell you? My advice has never been practical. Catch the water in your arms. Hug an armadillo. Tell each snowflake how you love it as it falls. Your dreams are fish that flash through the water. Be slippery. Be lucky.

Here's your fortune, listen: it's all too fast.

I'm Losing You

Static on the radio.
The nighttime road stretches before me
forbidding, shadows stark, drop-offs
uncertain. This might be our last

communication. I've started drifting.
There are lights ahead. I'm uncertain
what map I thought I was using.
Outlines of mountains, and beyond that,

that ancient red sun sinking
into the sea. What did you used to tell me?
You said I was all charisma
and no constitution. You said my anger

could light the sky on fire.
That night in the hospital
tied down with IVs, I told you
I wanted to see the ocean.
Now I've been gone so long

and what's left of me
isn't that great. I'd prefer
you remember me from photos.
You said, I'm losing you.
Keep the map I left you.

In a Plague Year, I Thought I Could Turn My Illness

into a character in a fairy tale, like a talking cat.
That way it wouldn't be the main event,
taking up space. It just turns on us and occasionally
merits conversation. Or beheading. I forget which.

I was tired of thinking about being sick.
Tired of hospitals, of needles, of measuring sticks
telling me how sick I was. Tired of turning on the news
to hear death tolls and how sick the world was,
this country, our neighbors.

I wanted an escape. I walked in the woods and
found birds, walked on the water and found otters.
These were not magical talking animals.
A pileated woodpecker hung upside down,
as if to say, "You think your life is hard?"

I wanted to put on silk shoes and a ball gown
and forget my cane and wheelchair. Forget
I could not run through the sprinkler.
In a fairy tale, there is always grim death around the corner,
so grab that prince and eat a sandwich, because you never know

when you're going to have to weave armor out of nettles
for your twelve swan brothers or spin straw into gold.
You never know what you'll be asked for.
We've given up so many things already.
Cultivate your own garden: that's Voltaire,

always giving us advice in disaster, a little like
a talking cat. So I take my shears and watering can,
I grow dahlias and sweet peas and an apple tree
where my illness can climb if it needs to.
I harvest tiny green apples no one eats.

I never want to hear the word "corona" again.
If I want a crown, I'll ask for it. My illness has curled
up around this poem and fallen asleep.
Look to the woods, where the smoke swirls on the horizon.
We should never trust a talking cat. Remember Alice.

In a Plague Year, I Found Foxes

all around. On islands, red fur, grey, dusky black,
shades of autumn leaves, eyes amber
and unafraid, standing in grasses, waiting for us.

I found the fox inside me,
curling up in twigs and fur,
my sharpened teeth and hunger.

I burrowed in to protect us from the plague,
but there was nowhere to run.
Like flames in the forest,

it was all around, lives going up in smoke.
I never left the forest. I trusted
only familiar paths, familiar smells:

dirt, trees, beetles. Berries that stained
our mouths. I drew poems in the dust.
I grew a tail, I left foxfur wherever I went.

I don't know how I will come back,
or if I will. Our burrow now littered
with bones and mushrooms, a home

or a place for the spirits of the dead.
I could never outrun death; it is coming
for us both. Enjoy the colors of this winter sunset,

the bare branches, the visits of other foxes,
their cries in the night, the softness
around us, the tenderness of endings.

Disintegration

At the end of the world, I sat in the dark waiting for you,
but you didn't come. You didn't save me.

At the end we are always alone, candles slowly
burning out, losing the flame for lack of oxygen.

You didn't tell me it would be like this. All of it
came back to me so clearly, shadows on the walls

playing out scenes from my childhood, from our wedding,
from days when I was full of hope. Every tree I planted,

every animal I ever loved. I wasn't as weak as I thought.
There was enough for this. The waves rolled in and out

at midnight, and there was a wild wind. I thought: I will
go out with the wind. Under my feet the ground was shifting.

I couldn't feel my feet. The stars were bright but there was no
moon. I was alone, and the night air smelled like salt and smoke.

I couldn't bear to say goodbye anyway. I could have sworn
there were daffodils, the green and yellow, the sap of spring,

though I knew it was November. Your mind plays tricks.
I could hear the band playing, something like The Cure,

and people dancing. And that wind. It could have blown me away.

At the End of Two Years of the Plague, You are Tired of the Word Resilience

Even as you dig and plant, as you search
the skyline for something, anything better,
as you snap pictures of pink rhododendron and jonquils.

You are tired of waiting for vaccines,
of loneliness, of the lack of laughter.
This quarantine has lasted far longer

than anyone expected, than even you
prepared for. Reserves run low. The winter
lasts and lasts, even while we're impatient

for spring, with its pretense of renewal.
The clouds hang low, your screens flicker
and buzz for attention, and you think

of all the signs singing "for your safety."
You try to remember the last time you felt safe.
Road rage is up. Starlings peck at each other

outside your window. The Snow Moon
rises but it's too cold to spend much time looking.
Resilience: you hear "Silence, slice, siren."

In the Second Year of the Plague, I Plant a Fig Tree

because I want to know what it's like to be new again,
Eden, with green figs and honey. It will be just you and me

and maybe a snake for company. Already the roses are growing
a thorn hedge around us. Listen to me: sing a new song,

burn rosemary and rose petals. We'll become
a city on a hill. We've paved the way with things we lost:

cake flour, lipstick, a discarded pile of masks,
smiling up at us like ghosts. We dreamed

of this day, but didn't remember how much it cost us.
We've already forgotten the way things were before the plague.

Nightclubs, sharing an appetizer with a friend, casual hugs,
even accidentally brushing a stranger's hand.

So we'll be born again, love, standing under this tree, new
and shiny as apples, free to make a new world, free of memory,

ignorant of God or virus, demon or machine, empty of knowledge
ready to start over, ready to start with a plate of green figs,

under the juice of the ripening moon,
ready to grow roots into the earth.

A Story for After a Pandemic

I want to tell you a story
about a future in which
we can touch each other again,

where children play outside
without masks, where the government
no longer patrols the streets

with weapons. We emerge like newborns,
blinking, the sun too bright to our artificial-light
adjusted eyes. We realize the beauty

again of oranges, their perfume. We crush
leaves in our fingers—mint, maple.
There is a rainbow visible on the tree line.

We will never again take for granted
a dance, a kiss, a crowd, we promise. A farmer's market
and candy apples, a county fair, kettle corn.

It's all miracles. We gather in small groups
and tell the stories; who we lost, what we
will remember. We light fires and bury the dead.

After the pandemic, we will rejoin
at the river's edge, at the waterfalls
and seasides, like animals. Praise the ocean,

the sky, the stars: what doesn't protect us,
what remains, what holds us together.

When I Thought I Was Dying

It was easy to love things. Birds, the flutter of branches,
my husband who always has to be right.

I thought, I will lose all of this. I hugged my cats more.
I watched less television, except for comedies, which drugged

me to sleep at night. Stupid 1950's sci-fi films, especially.
Maybe I loved them too. I loved poetry and wrote almost every day,

thinking, I do not have time to write. The lights would flicker
and threaten outages. How like our bodies these power lines are,

reliable until they are not: eaten by rats or rammed by cars at random.
You see how I thought everything was profound: my Netflix

recommendations, passing a woman on the street and smiling at each other.
I ate a lot more pancakes, something I hadn't done since childhood.

I thought, maybe there will be a miracle. Maybe I will have more time.
A temporary grant of extension. I will still do taxes and fill out forms

at the doctor's office. I will have time to be mad at traffic.
I will stop petting random dogs. I will have time to stop

noticing when the hummingbird or deer or Steller's jay pauses
to look in my eyes, that moment before. That's the thing

about having time. You miss so much.

Notes

"Self-Portrait as a Desert During a Superbloom" was inspired by an article from The Washington Post on April 13, 2017, titled: "California Superbloom So Prolific You Can See It From Space."

"This is the Darkest Timeline" refers to a common phrase in comic books and pop culture in which any multiverses and string theory result in one timeline that is the best and one that is the worst.

Acknowledgments

American Poetry Journal: "One More Attempt at Disaster Preparedness";

American Poetry Review: "Disintegration," "In the Second Year of the Plague, I Plant a Fig Tree";

Another Chicago Magazine: "Sitting by Yourself at the End of the World —I Mean, Year," "Lights Out";

Atlanta Review: "Grimoire";

Baltimore Review: "Planting Camellias as an Act of Resistance";

Barrelhouse: "Cancer Scare";

Bellevue Literary Review: "Some Nerve: a Nocturne";

Boulevard: "They Are Waiting," "Self-Portrait as Murder Mystery";

Cave Wall: "Self-Portrait as Wisteria on a May Night";

Cherry Tree: "Self-Portrait as Seismologist";

The Cincinnati Review: "Self-Portrait as Late August Evening";

Contrary Magazine: "April in Middle Age";

Diode: "Self-Portrait as Weather Report";

Fourth River: "Under a Blood Moon, I Get My Brain Scanned";

F(r)iction: "Self-Portrait as Mutant," "Where I Come From";

HWA Poetry Showcase Volume III: "Mutant Sonnets: Self-Portrait as Bad 1950's Science Fiction Movie";

Interfictions: "Serendipity";

Jet Fuel Review: "In the Movie of My Life," "In a Plague Year, I Found Foxes," "Not Dead but Post-Life";

Moon City Review: "Every Time I Take Another Cancer Test, I Feel the Universe Collapsing";

Natural Bridge: "Self-Portrait as MRI";

Nice Cage: "Failure, 2016";

Notre Dame Review: "On Being Told You're Dying, but Not Quite Believing It";

Plath Poetry Project: "Hospital Room, in April";

Ploughshares: "Irradiate";

Poetry: "Calamity";

Prairie Schooner: "Self-Portrait as February Morning," "When I Thought I Was Dying";

Rattle: "Self-Portrait as Escape Artist";

Rogue Agent: "Self-Portrait as Radioactive Girl," "July, in the Garden, I Feel Like Death";

Rosebud: "In the Time Between Sunspots," "The Summer of Bombs," "Supervillain, By the Sea, After the Summer of Bombs";

Seattle Review of Books: "This is the Darkest Timeline";

Shenandoah: "Introduction to Writer's Block";

Spoon River Poetry Review: "My Life is an Accident," "Mutant Sonnets: Signs of Spring on the Way to Medical Testing," "Self-Portrait as Desert During Superbloom";

StorySouth: "I Thought You Can't Go Home Again";

Sugar House Review: "I Can't Stop," "Meltdown";

The Tahoma Literary Review: "Flare";

Tinderbox: "When It All Falls Apart," "Almost April";

West Trestle Review: "In a Plague Year, I Held a Glass Baby";

Whale Road Review: "A Conspiracy of Ravens Began."

Thanks to the wonderful team at BOA Editions for their tremendous help, including careful editing by Peter Conners, Sandy Knight for the art and design work on the cover, and all kinds of work by Michelle Dashevsky and Genevieve Hartman. Thanks to the University of Washington's Whiteley Center for the residency during which some of this book was written. Thanks also to my friends who looked at earlier versions of this manuscript, including Kelli Russell Agodon, Steve Fellner, Tony Robinson, Lesley Wheeler, and my two most dedicated editors, my mother, Dr. Bettie Hall, and my husband, Glenn Gailey.

About the Author

Jeannine Hall Gailey is a writer with multiple sclerosis who served as the second Poet Laureate of Redmond, Washington. She's the author of six books of poetry including *Field Guide to the End of the World*, winner of the Moon City Book Prize and the Science Fiction Poetry Association's Elgin Award. She's also published the non-fiction book *PR for Poets: A Guidebook for Publicity and Marketing*. She has both a B.S. in Biology and an M.A. in English from the University of Cincinnati and an MFA from Pacific University. Her work has appeared in many journals, including *The American Poetry Review, Ploughshares,* and *Poetry.* Her web site is www.webbish6.com. She can be followed @webbish6 on Twitter and Instagram.

BOA Editions, Ltd. American Poets Continuum Series

No. 1 *The Fuhrer Bunker: A Cycle of Poems in Progress*
W. D. Snodgrass

No. 2 *She*
M. L. Rosenthal

No. 3 *Living With Distance*
Ralph J. Mills, Jr.

No. 4 *Not Just Any Death*
Michael Waters

No. 5 *That Was Then: New and Selected Poems*
Isabella Gardner

No. 6 *Things That Happen Where There Aren't Any People*
William Stafford

No. 7 *The Bridge of Change: Poems 1974–1980*
John Logan

No. 8 *Signatures*
Joseph Stroud

No. 9 *People Live Here: Selected Poems 1949–1983*
Louis Simpson

No. 10 *Yin*
Carolyn Kizer

No. 11 *Duhamel: Ideas of Order in Little Canada*
Bill Tremblay

No. 12 *Seeing It Was So*
Anthony Piccione

No. 13 *Hyam Plutzik: The Collected Poems*

No. 14 *Good Woman: Poems and a Memoir 1969–1980*
Lucille Clifton

No. 15 *Next: New Poems*
Lucille Clifton

No. 16 *Roxa: Voices of the Culver Family*
William B. Patrick

No. 17 *John Logan: The Collected Poems*

No. 18 *Isabella Gardner: The Collected Poems*

No. 19 *The Sunken Lightship*
Peter Makuck

No. 20 *The City in Which I Love You*
Li-Young Lee

No. 21 *Quilting: Poems 1987–1990*
Lucille Clifton

No. 22 *John Logan: The Collected Fiction*

No. 23 *Shenandoah and Other Verse Plays*
Delmore Schwartz

No. 24 *Nobody Lives on Arthur Godfrey Boulevard*
Gerald Costanzo

No. 25 *The Book of Names: New and Selected Poems*
Barton Sutter

No. 26 *Each in His Season*
W. D. Snodgrass

No. 27 *Wordworks: Poems Selected and New*
Richard Kostelanetz

No. 28 *What We Carry*
Dorianne Laux

No. 29 *Red Suitcase*
Naomi Shihab Nye

Colophon

BOA Editions, Ltd., a not-for-profit publisher of poetry
and other literary works, fosters readership and appreciation
of contemporary literature. By identifying, cultivating, and publishing both
new and established poets and selecting authors of unique literary talent,
BOA brings high-quality literature to the public.

Support for this effort comes from the sale of its publications, grant funding,
and private donations.

∴

*The publication of this book is made possible, in part,
by the special support of the following individuals:*

Anonymous
June C. Baker
Blue Flower Arts, LLC
Angela Bonazinga & Catherine Lewis
Rick Bursky
Christopher C. Dahl
James Long Hale
Margaret B. Heminway
Charles Hertrick & Joan Gerrity
Grant Holcomb
Kathleen Holcombe
Nora A. Jones
Paul LaFerriere & Dorrie Parini, *in honor of Bill Waddell*
Barbara Lovenheim
Joe McEleveny
Nocon & Associates, a private wealth advisory practice of
Ameriprise Financial Services LLC
Boo Poulin
John H. Schultz
William Waddell & Linda Rubel